CREATURES
WE CAN'T LIVE
WITH

We Need
PLANTS

SARAH MACHAJEWSKI

PowerKiDS press.

New York

Published in 2016 by The Rosen Publishing Group, Inc.
29 East 21st Street, New York, NY 10010

First Edition

Editor: Caitie McAneney
Book Design: Mickey Harmon

Photo Credits: Cover (image) Zoom Team/Shutterstock.com; cover, pp. 1, 3, 4, 6, 11, 15, 16–18, 21, 22–24 (background) Click Bestsellers/Shutterstock.com; pp. 4–5 (flowers), 5 (crops) AlinaMD/Shutterstock.com; p. 6 (maple leaf) Russel Shively/Shutterstock.com; p. 6 (pine leaves) Valentina Razumova/Shutterstock.com; p. 7 (sky) Elenamiv/Shutterstock.com; p. 7 (plant) Filipe B. Varela/Shutterstock.com; pp. 8–9 Monkey Business Images/Shutterstock.com; p. 10 Felix Mizioznikov/Shutterstock.com; pp. 12–13 Natalia Klenova/Shutterstock.com; p. 14 Justin Guariglia/age fotostock/Getty Images; p. 15 (cotton) Brzostowska/Shutterstock.com; p. 16 (willow bark) Kalcutta/Shutterstock.com; p. 16 (periwinkle) SweetCrisis/Shutterstock.com; p. 16 (aloe vera) anyauvanova/Shutterstock.com; p. 17 (hemlock) Aleksandr Stepanov/Shutterstock.com; p. 18 (fern fossil) Paul B. Moore/Shutterstock.com; p. 19 bikeriderlondon/Shutterstock.com; p. 20 KidStock/Blend Images/Getty Images; p. 22 (grains) Chiociolla/Shutterstock.com; p. 22 (flax) Wolfgang Kruck/Shutterstock.com.

Library of Congress Cataloging-in-Publication Data

Machajewski, Sarah, author.
 We need plants / Sarah Machajewski.
     pages cm. — (Creatures we can't live without)
 Includes bibliographical references and index.
 ISBN 978-1-4994-0983-3 (pbk.)
 ISBN 978-1-4994-1025-9 (6 pack)
 ISBN 978-1-4994-1042-6 (library binding)
 1. Plants—Juvenile literature. I. Title. II. Series: Creatures we can't live without.
 QK49.M178 2015
 580—dc23
                        2015009239

Manufactured in the United States of America

CPSIA Compliance Information: Batch #WS15PK: For Further Information contact Rosen Publishing, New York, New York at 1-800-237-9932

CONTENTS

VERY IMPORTANT PLANTS

Look around you. What kind of plants do you see? You may see a potted flower in your bedroom. Outside, there may be an area of grass or a giant tree. You may even spot farmland with plants as far as the eye can see. All these plants are different, but they're equally important to our lives.

People use plants for everything, including food, clothing, and **shelter**. We also use them to make **medicine** and tools. The list doesn't stop there. We need plants for almost everything. Read on to see why plants are living things we can't live without.

Plants use sunlight for **energy**. They're a source of energy for living things that eat them.

WHAT'S A PLANT?

Plants are living, multicellular **organisms**. That means they're made of many cells. However, they don't have a brain. Plant cells contain cellulose, which is matter that makes them stiff. They stay in one place as they grow, and they make their own food. This **process** is called photosynthesis (foh-toh-SIHN-thuh-suhs). We'll learn about that later.

There are hundreds of thousands of plant species, or kinds, in the world. New ones are discovered all the time. Every plant looks different, but almost all of them have roots, a stem, leaves, and flowers. Sometimes, flowers make fruit. People depend on the fruit plants make for food.

CREATURE CLUE

Some leaves, such as maple leaves, are flat and wide. Others, such as pine leaves, are thin and long. Big or small, leaves help plants make food.

PINE LEAVES

MAPLE LEAVES

FLOWERS

LEAVES

STEM

ROOTS

This image shows the parts of a plant.
Each part plays an important **role** in
plants'—and our—lives.

PLANTS ARE EVERYWHERE

Plants are found everywhere in the world. They grow around our homes, but they're also found on beaches, deserts, plains, mountains, and even in the sea. However, the plants that grow in one of these places may not be able to grow in another.

Plants grow where they're best able to survive. Their survival depends on climate, or average weather over a period of time, and also history. Plants growing in an area today likely grew there many thousands of years ago. Throughout history, people have depended on the plants that grow near them.

CREATURE CLUE

When Europeans first came to America, they didn't know how to grow corn because it wasn't found in Europe. Native Americans had to teach them how to grow and use it.

Straw is the part of grain plants, such as wheat and rye, that people don't eat. People who grow grain plants for food use the straw in other ways, such as making hats, shoes, rope, paper, and more.

What's the number-one reason we need plants?
They give us oxygen! Without it, people and
animals couldn't survive.

BREATHING AND EATING

Plants eat and breathe, but the way they do it is different from the way we do it. Plants are stuck in one place, so they can't move around to find food. Instead, they use photosynthesis to make their own.

Plants need sunlight, water, and air to go through photosynthesis. Plants take in sunlight through their leaves. Tiny holes in their leaves "breathe" in carbon dioxide, a gas in the air, and their roots take in water and **nutrients** from the soil. Photosynthesis uses the sun's energy to turn these things into sugar, which plants use as food. It also creates oxygen, which is a gas we need to breathe.

CREATURE CLUE

The energy plants take in from the sun is passed to the animals and people who eat the plants. A food chain shows the flow of energy from plants to the animals and people who eat them.

FOOD FOR ALL

People and animals need food to live, but they can't make their own like plants do. So, we eat plants instead. Plants are a major food source for many living things. They're the reason we have any food at all. Even the meat we eat, such as chickens and pigs, once ate corn, oats, or grass.

Long ago, people traveled in search of food. Then, people decided to start planting and growing their own food. This allowed them to stay in one place, which created cities and then entire **civilizations**. Without plants, we might not live in towns and cities today.

CREATURE CLUE

People started growing plants for food around 12,000 years ago. Before that, people had to hunt and gather all the food they needed. Agriculture, or farming, gave people control over what they ate.

Plants are also used to flavor food. **Herbs** and spices come from plants. They can make a dish taste spicy, sweet, smoky, earthy, and more.

Plants have long been used to dye, or color, clothing. People crushed berries, leaves, and flowers to create beautiful colors.

CREATING CLOTHING

Where do clothes come from? You may say "the store," but many come from plants first. Plants give us **material** to make different kinds of clothes. Clothes are important because they keep us warm, dry, and safe from bad weather.

Today, cotton is the most commonly used plant for making clothes. It's very soft and is used to make shirts, socks, pants, dresses, and more. Linen, another **fiber**, comes from a plant called flax. Linen is very light. People wear it in the summer to keep cool. Even leather and wool, which are materials that come from animals, depend on plants—cows and sheep eat them to survive!

CREATURE CLUE

Cotton plants are used for more than clothing. Cottonseeds are used to make oil for cooking. The fuzz on the plant, called linter, is used to make plastic, paper, and furniture.

PLANT MEDICINE

You may take medicine when you get sick or hurt. This wouldn't be possible without plants. Thousands of years ago, people discovered they could use plants to make them feel better. Native Americans once chewed on parts of the willow plant as a pain-killer. Chemicals in cinchona tree bark were used to fight a serious illness called malaria.

All the plants you see here can help us feel better in different ways.

PERIWINKLE PLANT

WILLOW BARK

ALOE VERA PLANT

Aloe plants are used to help sunburns feel better. The periwinkle plant is used in medicines that treat some kinds of cancer. **Vitamins** that come from plants help our bodies stay healthy. Today, scientists are always looking for new ways to use plants to make medicine.

HEMLOCK

CREATURE CLUE

While some plants are very helpful, others contain chemicals that can make people feel sick. Some plants, such as hemlock, can even kill people if they're eaten. Never eat or use a plant without first finding out if it's safe.

BUILDING BLOCKS

If there's one plant people can't live without, it's trees. They're a major building material. Wood is used to build homes and buildings of all sizes. Many smaller objects, such as furniture and toys, are made of wood, too. Trees are also used to make paper and pencils. The list of objects made from trees is very long.

Another material we couldn't live without is coal. Coal is a **fossil fuel** that gives us power and helps us heat our homes. Coal formed from remains of plants that lived millions of years ago. Even plants from the past help us!

CREATURE CLUE

Coal is made of the remains of plant parts, trees, and plants called ferns. Sometimes, you can see whole plant parts in certain kinds of coal.

FERN FOSSIL

Coal is a good source of power and heat, but some people worry that we're using too much of it. Once it runs out, it can't be replaced. Also, burning coal pollutes the air.

SAVE OUR PLANTS!

People use plants in countless ways. However, we must be careful of how much we use. Every time we cut down a tree or pick a crop of plants, we need to be careful to replace the plants and keep the natural surroundings in mind. When we pollute the air, water, and ground, it hurts the plants that need them to live and grow.

We can help plants by not polluting and by not using more plants than we need. These are some ways to make sure plants are around for many years to come. Plants are some of the most important things on Earth. We can't live without them!

Planting a tree can create shade, lessen air pollution, make homes for animals, and recycle water.

Plants and Their Many Uses!

Check out this chart to find out how each plant can serve one or many important purposes.

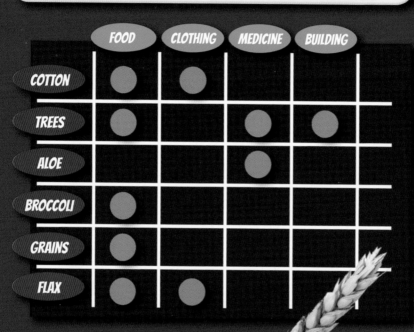

	FOOD	CLOTHING	MEDICINE	BUILDING
COTTON	●	●		
TREES	●		●	●
ALOE			●	
BROCCOLI	●			
GRAINS	●			
FLAX	●	●		

FLAX

GRAINS

GLOSSARY

civilization: An organized society.

energy: The power to do work.

fiber: A thread made from plant tissue.

fossil fuel: Matter formed from the remains of plants and animals over millions of years that is burned for power.

herb: A low-growing plant used to add flavor to food.

material: Something such as cloth or wood that is used to make something.

medicine: A drug taken to make a sick person well.

nutrient: Something taken in by a plant or animal that helps it grow and stay healthy.

organism: A living thing.

process: A series of steps.

role: The part something plays.

shelter: A place to live or stay.

vitamin: Matter important in small amounts for the health of animals.

INDEX

WEBSITES

Due to the changing nature of Internet links, PowerKids Press has developed an online list of websites related to the subject of this book. This site is updated regularly. Please use this link to access the list: www.powerkidslinks.com/cwcl/plan